Ultimate Cars

A.T. McKenna
ABDO Publishing Company

visit us at
www.abdopub.com

Published by Abdo Publishing Company, 4940 Viking Drive, Edina, Minnesota 55435.
Copyright © 2000 by Abdo Consulting Group, Inc. International copyrights reserved in all
countries. No part of this book may be reproduced in any form without written permission from
the publisher.

Printed in the United States.

Cover and Interior Photo credits: A/P Wideworld Photos, Corbis, David Gooley, SuperStock

Library of Congress Cataloging-in-Publication Data

McKenna, A. T.
    Ferrari / A. T. McKenna.
        p. cm. -- (Ultimate cars)
    Includes index.
    Summary: Surveys the history of the Ferrari and its designs, engines, and performance.
      ISBN 1-57765-123-5
    1. Ferrari automobile -- Juvenile literature. [1. Ferrari automobile.] I. Title. II. Series.
TL215.F47M35 2000
629.222'1--dc21

                      98-13021
                      CIP
                      AC

Contents

Italy's Sports Car

Ferrari is the great fantasy car—dreamed about by many, owned by few. Ferraris have been some of the greatest race cars seen on the world's racing circuits, including Formula One. Ferraris are also some of the fastest cars on the street.

A Ferrari is considered to be a sports car. A sports car is fast and has a sporty look. It is designed for the fun of driving. Most sports cars have only two seats. Many times the word *sport* is used in the name of the car. For example, *SS* stands for "Sport Sedan" and *GS* stands for "Grand Sport."

Ferrari sports cars are recognized by their yellow and black prancing horse logo. It dates back to an Italian cavalry regiment in 1682. The logo is called *Cavallino Rampante* in Italian.

Opposite page: The bright yellow and black Ferrari logo is easy to recognize on Ferrari race cars.

Enzo Ferrari

Enzo Ferrari test-drives a 1924 Alpha Romeo.

Ferraris were created by a man named Enzo Ferrari. He was born on February 18, 1898, just outside of Modena, Italy. His father owned a metal shop and motor repair business, so Enzo was surrounded by machines. When he was a boy, Enzo wanted to be a race car driver.

During World War I, Enzo served in the Italian army. But when the war was over, he returned to his passion: sports cars. He got a job with a car company as a test driver. Next, Alfa Romeo hired him as a race car driver. Later, he became an Alfa Romeo engineer and manager of the company's racing team.

In 1939, Enzo resigned from Alfa Romeo after 20 years. Enzo wanted to create his own cars. But, when he left Alfa Romeo, he agreed not to build or race cars under his own name for four years. So, his first car was just called Model 815.

By 1945, Enzo was free to build cars under his own name. But instead, he decided to manufacture machine tools. He thought it was a more stable business than building sports cars.

Enzo changed his mind on Christmas Eve in 1946, when Luigi Chinetti payed him a visit. Chinetti was a race car driver who had worked with Enzo at Alfa Romeo. Chinetti had become a U.S. citizen in 1946. He knew there was a market for European sports cars in the U.S. So, the two men decided to start a business.

They introduced the public to the first Ferrari sports cars in Maranello, Italy, on May 11, 1947. Two models were shown: a two-seat Spyder Corsa and a roadster. Each had a V-12 engine designed by Gioacchino Colombo. They were both called Type 125S sports cars.

A Type 125S Spyder Corsa

After the first Ferraris appeared, Enzo kept designing cars. During his long career, he created some of the world's fastest and most beautiful cars.

Famous Ferrari People

There are many people at Ferrari who helped build Italy's famous sports car. The founder of Ferrari is, of course, Enzo Ferrari. He started building cars under his own name in 1946.

Ferrari relied on his friend and partner, Luigi Chinetti. Chinetti gave Ferrari many ideas for the early cars. Chinetti was also a race car driver who had much success racing Ferraris. He was in charge of selling Ferraris in the United States.

Gioacchino Colombo designed engines for Ferrari. Colombo created many of Ferrari's V-12 engines. These were Enzo's favorite kind of engine.

Another engine designer was Enzo's son, Dino. Dino designed V-8, V-6, and some V-4 engines. In 1956, Dino died from muscular dystrophy. Enzo named the Dino 206 model in honor of his son. It had a V-6 engine, Dino's favorite kind.

Carlo Felice Bianchi Anderloni was one of Ferrari's first designers. He designed the great 166 Touring Barchetta.

Enzo Ferrari

Ferrari's Carrozzerias

Enzo Ferrari designed many of his own cars and engines. But, most of the body design and construction was done elsewhere. The car bodies were built by *carrozzerias*, which means "coach builders" in Italian. The car body is made of panels that fit over the chassis, or frame. The body is handcrafted most of the time. The two *carrozzerias* Ferrari used most often were Pininfarina and Vignale.

Pininfarina was Ferrari's chief body designer for many years. Battisa Farina started the company in Turin, Italy. The company was first called Stabilimenti Farina. In 1950 the name of the company changed to Pinin Farina and then Pininfarina.

Farina designed the body of the Ferrari 410 Superamerica.

Farina worked with Ferrari for many years, designing bodies for the beautiful cars. Farina designed and built the 011 S. It was the first convertible Ferrari. Farina also designed the famous 365 GTB/4 Daytona. And Farina designed the 410 Superamerica, one of the world's most dynamic road car designs.

Carrozzeria Vignale was the other main body designer for Ferrari. The company was also located in Turin, Italy. In the early 1950s, Vignale became famous for its Ferrari body designs. Vignale designed some of the Ferraris made especially for the United States market, including the 375 America. Vignale-designed cars won many auto races, especially the famous Mille Miglia in Italy. These cars were sleek and fast!

Vignale designed the body for the 375 America, which was made especially for the U.S.

Creating a Car

Building a car is not an easy task. It takes many people, from designers and engineers to mechanics and assembly line crews. First, the design department must come up with an idea of how the car should look. The designer usually draws several versions of the car before it is accepted.

Then, designers use wood and foam to make a frame. The frame is the actual size of the car. Warm clay is laid on the frame to make a life-sized model of the car.

Today, computers are often used to design cars. Automobile designers use Computer Aided Design (CAD) techniques once the basic shape of the car is decided upon. The clay model of the car is scanned into the computer. The designer can then change the design with the touch of a button.

The design of the car must be approved by the executives of the company. Once it is approved, engineers work with mechanics to build a prototype.

A prototype is an early version of the car. All the parts on the prototype are tested for strength and quality. The prototype is tested on a race track or on the street to see how it handles. It is displayed at car shows to get people's responses before the actual cars are produced.

After much research is done on the prototype, executives at the company decide whether or not to build the car. If the car is going to be built, changes are made based on the results of the testing and the responses from people who saw it. Usually, the actual car does not look very much like the prototype.

Next, it is time to build the car for the public. Most cars go through an assembly line when being built. An assembly line is a system used to produce many kinds of products, such as cars. Each worker has a specific job to do.

A prototype of the Ferrari Dino

Assembly-line workers line up in rows and perform their jobs as the car moves down the line. One worker may put in the steering wheel, while another installs the engine.

In Ferrari's history, most of the cars were handbuilt one at a time. They didn't go through a large assembly line. But some models, such as the Dino and the Testarossa, were produced on an assembly line. This allowed Ferrari to produce thousands of cars instead of a few hundred.

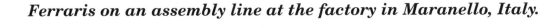
Ferraris on an assembly line at the factory in Maranello, Italy.

**An engineer works on an engine at the Ferrari factory
in Maranello, Italy.**

Ferrari Timeline

Type 125S

The 166 Touring Barchetta

The Dino

The Boxer

The Testarossa

The F40

Barchettas & Cabriolets

The Ferrari factory has produced many cars for competition in auto races. But it was Luigi Chinetti who convinced Enzo to offer cars for both the road and the track. So Ferrari introduced the 166 Touring Barchetta in 1949.

The Barchetta had a long hood and short rear end. It also had an oval-shaped grille, which became a Ferrari trait for years. The car was constructed of small, lightweight steel tubes with body panels attached.

The engine was a V-12, which produced 140 horsepower at 6,600 rpm. The number after *V* stands for how many cylinders the engine has. Horsepower is the amount of power the engine has. The initials *rpm* stand for revolutions per minute. This means that while the engine is running, it goes through the same sequence of events thousands of times per minute to keep the fuel flowing through it.

The Barchetta was called a touring car, which is a cross between a race car and a road car. It could be used as either. Most of the Barchettas were used as race cars. Usually they were painted metallic red, a Ferrari tradition. Between 1948 and 1953, Barchettas won 80 victories in European races.

Almost 50 years after its debut, the 166 Touring Barchetta is still one of the most admired Ferraris.

Enzo Ferrari knew he needed to build a car for people who didn't race cars. So he asked Stabilimenti Farina to build a convertible road car. The 011 S cabriolet was built in 1949. Cabriolet is another word for convertible. This car looked like the Barchetta without the roof. It was the first Ferrari convertible.

People at a car show admire the 166 Touring Barchetta. In Italian, the world barchetta *means "small boat."*

The Dynamic Dinos

Enzo Ferrari's son Dino was a great engine designer. His best engine models were V-6 engines. After Dino died, Enzo built a 1956 model in honor of his son. It was called the Dino 206.

The Dino 206 was low and sleek. Its engine was mounted in the middle of the car instead of the front. This is called mid-engined. This balanced the car's weight better. Enzo did not put the prancing horse logo on this model. Instead, he had his son's name placed on the hood.

The Dino models were not as fast as other Ferraris. But, they were lower in price. This made Dinos very popular cars.

In order to keep up with the orders, Enzo made a deal with a large Italian car company called Fiat. Ferrari used Fiat's large factories to build thousands of Dinos.

In 1976, Enzo changed the engines in the Dino to a V-8. It gave the Dino more speed and power. He also put the Ferrari logo and name on the cars. The Dino influenced the famous 308, 328, and 348 Ferrari models.

A Ferrari Dino

The Boxer

In the early 1970s, Ferrari introduced a mid-engined Ferrari — the 365 GT4 Berlinetta Boxer.

The Boxer got its name from its flat V-12 engine. Since the engine was flat, the cylinders lay pointed toward each other. When the pistons moved up and down in the cylinders, they looked like two boxers fighting.

The body of the Boxer was a mixture of materials. The main body of the Boxer was made of steel. The hood, doors, and trunk were made of aluminum. The lower body panels were made of fiberglass.

The Boxer was a fast car, speeding up to 188 mph (302 km/h). This speed caused some problems. For example, the boxer went so fast that sometimes it lifted off the ground. Another problem was with the mid-engine placement. Heat from the engine made the inside of the car very warm, especially in the summer.

The 365 Boxer was never sold in the United States. Its design did not meet the United State's strict safety and pollution laws.

In 1976, the 365 Boxer was replaced by the 512 Berlinetta Boxer. It was almost identical to the 365. The

512 is still one of the most desirable of all Ferraris.

The evolution of the Boxer models has led to some of the most famous Ferraris, including the 308 GTB and the GTS.

Ferrari Boxer

The Testarossa

Ferrari introduced the world to the Testarossa at the 1984 Paris Auto Show. The word *testarossa* means "red head" in Italian. The car received this name because the tops of the engine pistons were painted bright red.

The Testarossa, called TR by many, was built from 1985 until 1996. Names of Testarossa models included the 512TR and the 512M.

The Testarossa's engine was a flat V-12, just like the Boxer. The engine boasted nearly 400 horsepower. The top speed of the Testarossa has been clocked at 196 mph (315 km/h)!

Pininfarina designed and built the Testarossa body. The body was made of aluminum, but the roof and doors were made of steel. Ferrari installed high-tech machines to make sure the Testarossa's parts fit together perfectly. This allowed Ferrari to build more cars in less time.

The Testarossa was very wide. It stretched more than 6.5 feet (2 m) from side to side. It was also longer than previous Ferraris, allowing plenty of room for tall drivers.

The Ferrari Testarossa

The Wild Ride - F40

The F40 was introduced to celebrate Ferrari's fortieth anniversary. The *F* stood for Ferrari, and the *40* stood for the number of years that Ferraris had been built. The F40 was the last car Enzo Ferrari designed before he died. It was built from 1987 until 1992.

The F40's body was made of Kevlar. The windows on the F40 were made of plastic and they could slide out. The F40 had no door handles. Instead, the car had a rope on the inside that the driver pulled when he or she wanted to open the door.

The car weighed 2,680 pounds (1,216 kg) when its 32-gallon (121 lt) gas tank was full. The F40 had a sticker price of $250,000. But, the price of the F40s soared to $1 million as people traded them. About 1,350 F40s were produced. Only 200 were exported to the United States.

The F40 was fast. It was more like a race car than a road car. The F40 was the first non-racing Ferrari to break the 200 mph (322 km/h) mark. The factory quoted a top speed of 203.4 mph (327 km/h)!

Ferrari Racing

Ferrari started out building only race cars.

Ferrari cars have a long racing history. They have won more than 4,000 races, which is more than any other car.

In 1952, Ferrari went to America to compete in the famous Indianapolis 500. The car he brought to compete was called the Ferrari Special. The driver was the great Alberto Ascari. Ascari's speeds during practice impressed the other drivers who thought he would win.

On race day, the #12 Ferrari lined up for the start. Ascari surged through the pack at the green flag. Soon, the wire spokes on one of the wheels weakened and the wheel collapsed. Ascari drove off the track unhurt, but out of the race. It was the first and only try Ferrari had at the Indianapolis 500.

Ferrari cars have competed in many other races. But, they have had the most success in Formula One races. Today, Michael Schumacher, one of the top Formula One racers, drives a Ferrari. He finished the 1997 Formula One Championship in second place behind Jacques Villeneuve.

Over the years, Ferrari has sponsored cars for many famous Formula One race car drivers. They include Mario Andretti, Phil Hill, Dan Gurney, Gilles Villeneuve, and Nigel Mansell.

Michael Schumacher drives his Ferrari to victory at the 1999 San Marino Formula One Grand Prix, giving Ferrari its first victory at San Marino since 1983.

Glossary

cylinder - the chamber in the engine where fuel is burned.

carrozzeria - companies that built the bodies of the cars for Ferrari.

chassis - the frame of the car. The chassis is like a skeleton of the car.

Computer Aided Design (CAD) - computer software that allows a person to design a car by using a computer.

debut - the first public appearance.

executive - a person who directs or manages a company's affairs.

export - to send goods to another country for sale or trade.

fiberglass - a durable, nonflammable material that is made from fine threads of glass.

Formula One - a kind of race in which people drive single-seat cars. The insides of the cars have no luxuries, only the basic instruments required for driving.

Indianapolis 500 - a famous race that began in 1911. The race takes place every Memorial Day weekend in Indianapolis, Indiana.

Kevlar - a carbon composite material used to make the body of cars. Kevlar is stronger than steel or fiberglass.

Mille Miglia - a famous auto race in Italy. Ferraris frequently won the Mille Miglia.

muscular dystrophy - a disease where a person's muscles slowly weaken and waste away.

piston - a disk that fits closely inside an engine's cylinder and moves back and forth.

roadster - a open car with a single seat for two or more people, often there is a rumble seat or luggage compartment in the rear.

scan - to pass an electric beam over an image. The beam converts the image to electronic properties, which allows the scanned image to be altered or transferred by a computer.

Internet Sites

Ferrari Official Web Site
http://www.ferrari.it/menu/frameeng.html

This is the official Ferrari Web Site. It has information about the history of Ferrari cars. And it keeps readers up-to-date on new models, racing, and breaking Ferrari news.

Ferrari Club of America
http://www.ferrariclubofameria.org

This site is provided by the largest Ferrari club in the world! This site has great photos, racing news, and links to other great Ferrari sites.

These sites are subject to change. Go to your favorite search engine and type in "Ferrari" for more sites.

Index